# PUPIL
# TEXTBOOK
# 1A

Ooogol

Noogol

Googol

Koogol

Toogol

Zoogol

Consultant and author
Dr Fong Ho Kheong

**Authors**
Chelvi Ramakrishnan and Bernice Lau Pui Wah

**UK consultants**
Carole Skinner, Simon d'Angelo and Elizabeth Gibbs

# Introduction

**Inspire Maths** is a comprehensive, activity-based programme designed to provide pupils with a firm foundation in maths and to develop the creative and critical thinking skills to become fluent problem solvers.

**Inspire Maths** makes learning maths fun and rewarding through the use of engaging illustrations and games that help to reinforce and consolidate learning.

## For the teacher:

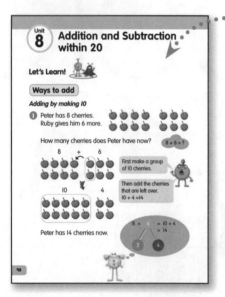

Use the engaging and highly scaffolded **Let's Learn!** to introduce concepts. Integrated questions allow for immediate assessment and consolidation of concepts learnt.

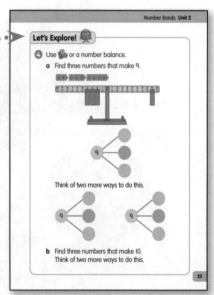

Carry out investigative activities in **Let's Explore!** These allow pupils to apply concepts learnt.

Challenge pupils to solve non-routine questions by applying relevant heuristics and thinking skills in **Put On Your Thinking Caps!**

## For the parent/guardian:

Build home-school links and make maths come alive by using the tips in Home Maths to help children apply mathematical concepts to daily life.

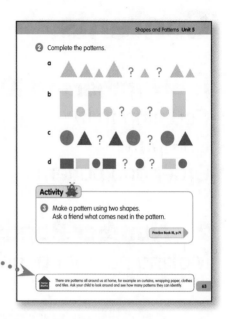

## For the pupil:

Enjoy **Inspire Maths** with your friends. Explore your learning through activities and games.

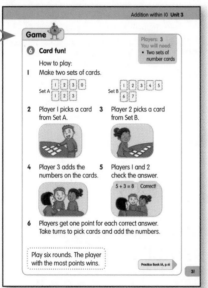

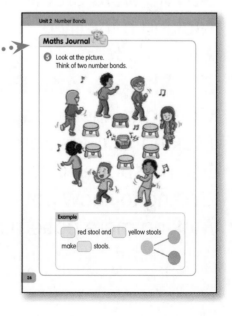

Share what you have learnt, create your own questions and become aware of your own mathematical thinking in your  Maths Journal .

# Contents

# Numbers to 10

## Let's Learn!

**Counting to 10**

Point with your finger and count.

**1**
one

**2**
two

**3**
three

**4**
four

**5**
five

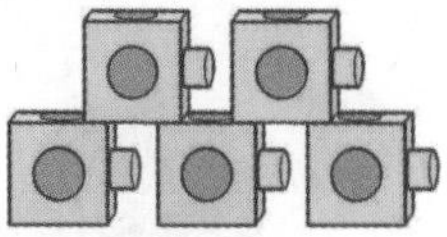

**6**
six

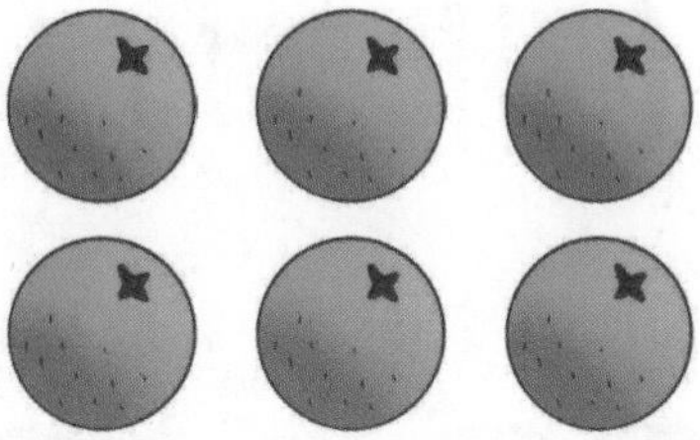

**7**
seven

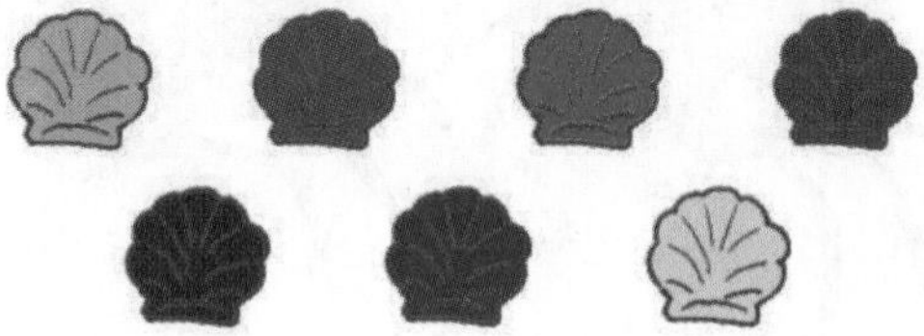

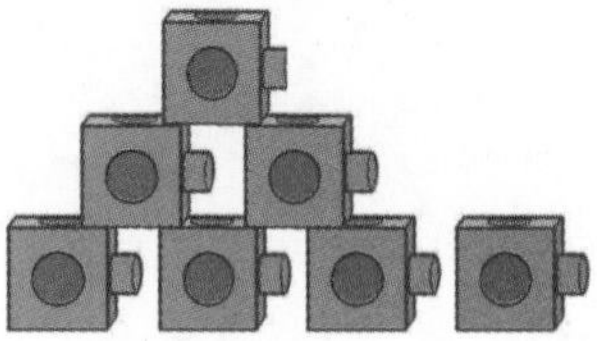

**8**
eight

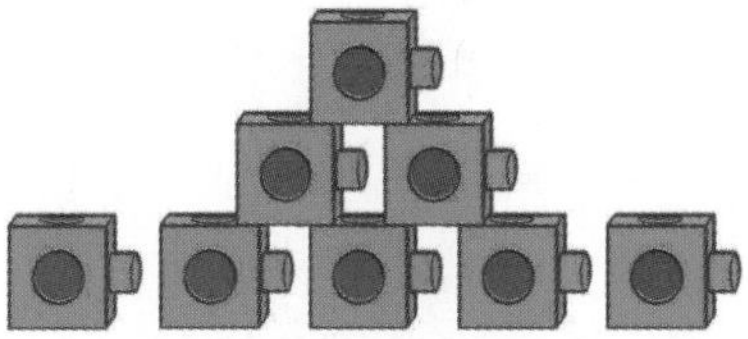

**9**
nine

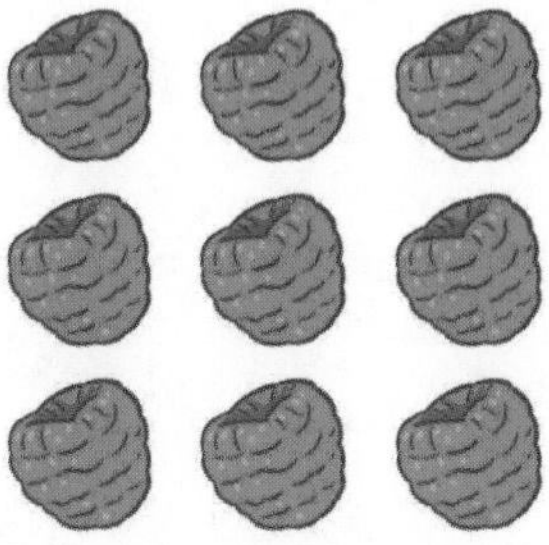

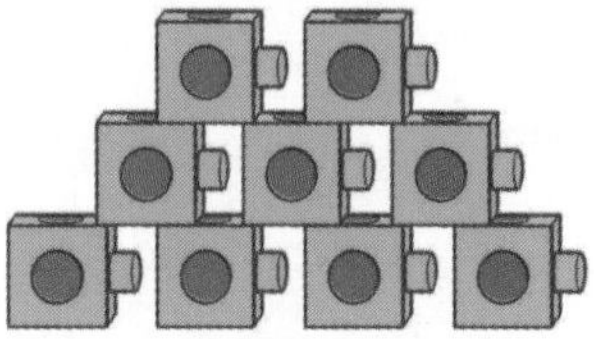

**10**
ten

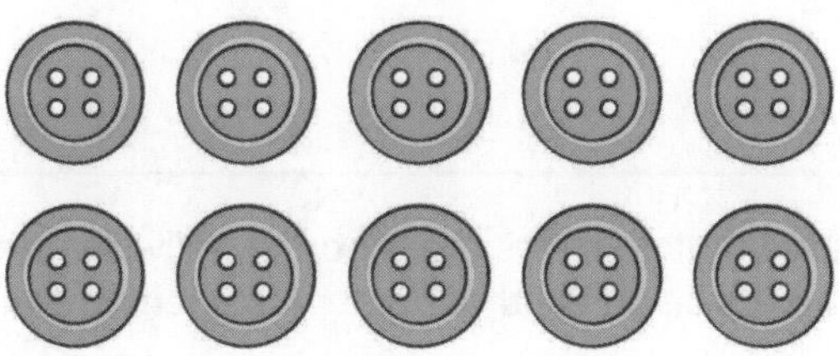

**2** How many spiders are there?

three 3

two 2

one I

zero 0

## Activity

**3** **a** Count the things. How many are there?

**b** Work in pairs.

Show your partner 10 🔲.

Show your partner 10 🔲.

Show your partner any 10 things around you.

**4** Count. Write in numbers and in words.

 **Home Maths** Make a fruit salad with your child. Ask them to count each piece of fruit you use.

**5** Count the things in the picture.
How many are there?

## Game

**Players: 3**

**6** **Hit 10!**

How to play:
Take turns to count on by 1, 2 or 3. Count on to 10.

**1** Player 1 starts counting from 1.

**2** Player 2 counts on.

1, 2

3, 4, 5

**3** Player 3 counts on.

6, 7, 8

9, 10. I win!

The player who says 10 wins!

Practice Book IA, p.5

# Let's Learn!

## Compare

**1** Match and compare.

There are 4 children.
There are 4 apples.
The number of children and the number of apples are
**the same**.

**2** Match and compare.

There are **more** children **than** apples.
There are **fewer** apples **than** children.

Match and compare.
Say if there are **more** or **fewer**.

**3**

There are [  ] socks than shoes.

There are [  ] shoes than socks.

**4**

There are [  ] cats than fish.

There are [  ] dogs than fish.

More or fewer?

## Activity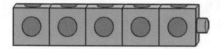

**5** This is a number train.

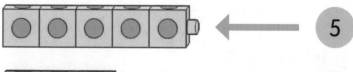

**1** Make a number train with more than 3 .
How many  are there in your train?

**2** Make a number train with fewer than 3 .
How many  are there in your train?

**3** Make a number train with more than 7 .
How many  are there in your train?

**4** Make a number train with fewer than 7 .
How many  are there in your train?

**6** Count and compare.

 ← 5

← 3

5 is **greater than** 3.
3 is **smaller than** 5.

**7** Count and compare.

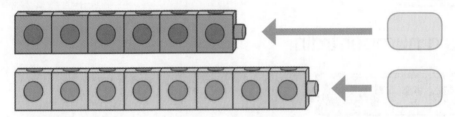

[  ] is greater than [  ].

[  ] is smaller than [  ].

**Activity**

**8** Make number trains using

**a**  4 [ ]

**b**  9 [ ]

Which number is greater? [  ]

Which number is smaller? [  ]

**9** Which number is greater? [  ]

8   or   5

**10** Which number is smaller? [  ]

6   or   9

Practice Book IA, p.13

# Let's Learn!

## Order and pattern

**1** Jack makes this pattern:

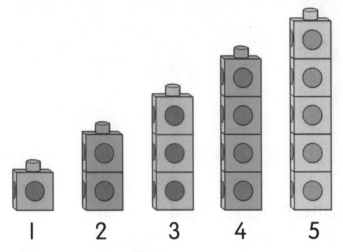

How many 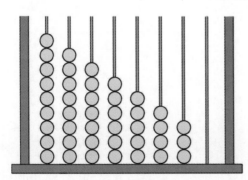 come next in the pattern?

1, 2, 3, 4, 5, **6**

6 come next in the pattern.

**2** Ella makes a pattern with beads.

How many beads come next in the pattern?

## Activity

3 Use 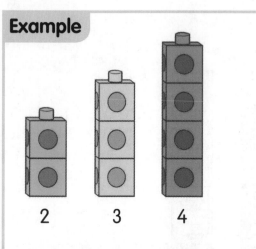 to make a set of towers.

**Example**

2    3    4

This shows a pattern from 2 to 4.

Use to show:

**a** a pattern from 4 to 7

**b** a pattern from 9 to 6

4 Count to find the next number.

I, 2, 3, 4, ⬚

**5** Complete the number patterns.

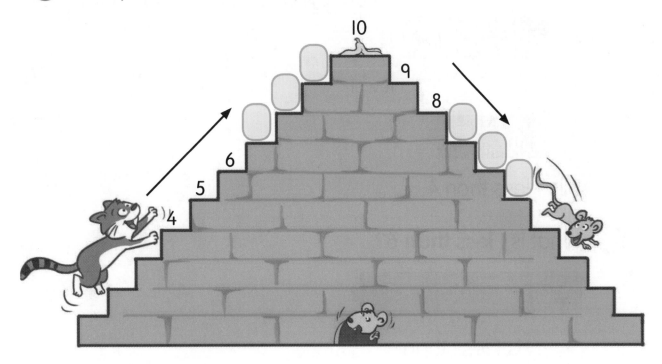

**6** What is 1 **more than** 3?

3

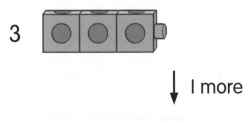

↓ 1 more

4

4 is 1 more than 3.

**7** What is 1 **more than** 6?

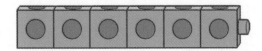

is 1 more than 6.

**8** What is I **less than** 4?

4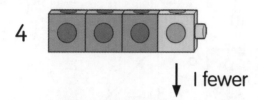

↓ I fewer

3

3 is I less than 4.

**9** What is I **less than** 6?

[ ] is I less than [ ].

**10** Complete the number patterns.

**a** 2, 3, 4, [ ], [ ], 7, 8

**b** 10, 9, [ ], [ ], [ ], 5, 4

Practice Book IA, p.19

## Maths Journal

**II** Which of these sentences are correct?

**a** A bicycle has 2 wheels.

**b** A triangle has 3 sides.

**c** 7 is smaller than 5.

**d** 8 is I less than 9.

## Maths Journal

**12** Write about the picture
using the numbers 1 to 10.

**Example**

There are 6 chairs.

## Put On Your Thinking Caps!

**13** Look at these number discs.

7   3   2   6   10   9   4   5   1   8

Put each disc in the correct box.

| Numbers smaller than 5 | Numbers from 5 to 7 | Numbers greater than 7 |
|---|---|---|
|  |  |  |

What can you say about the colours of the
discs in each group?

Practice Book 1A, p.23    Practice Book 1A, p.24

# Unit 2 — Number Bonds

**Let's Learn!**

**Making number bonds**

**Activity**

1. **a** You will need .
   Put the cubes into two groups.

**Example**

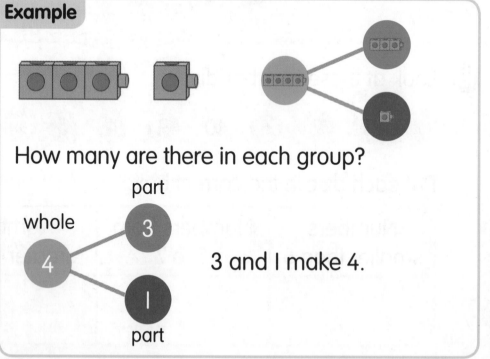

How many are there in each group?

whole

part

4

3

1

part

3 and 1 make 4.

22

## Activity

**b** What other numbers make 4?

[　] and [　] make 4. • • • • 4

[　] and [　] make 4. • • • • 4

**2** **a** Put  into two groups.

How many cubes are there in each group?

[　] and [　] make 5. • • • • 5

**b** What other numbers make 5?

[　] and [　] make 5. • • • • 5

[　] and [　] make 5. • • • • 5

## Activity

**3** **a** Make number bonds of 7 with a number balance.

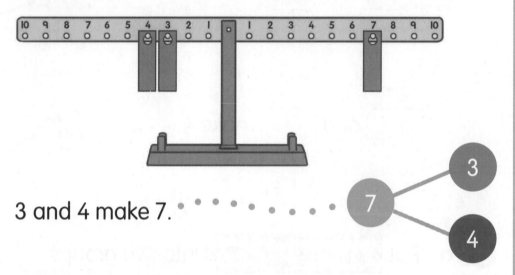

3 and 4 make 7.

**b** What other numbers make 7?

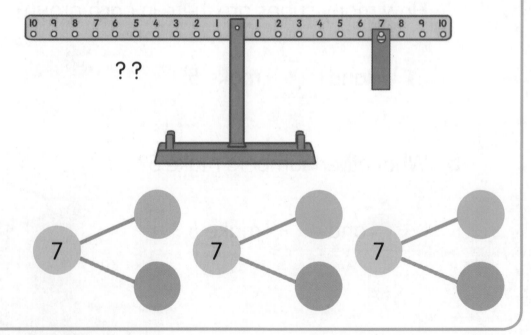

Practice Book IA, pp. 25, 29 and 31

## Let's Explore!

4 Use 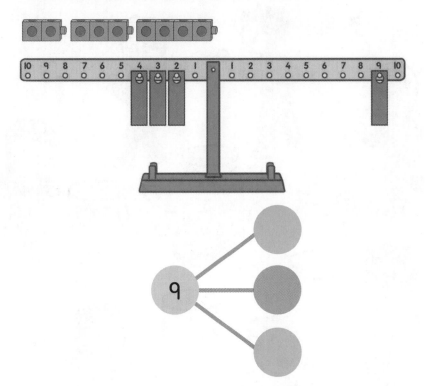 or a number balance.

a Find three numbers that make 9.

Think of two more ways to do this.

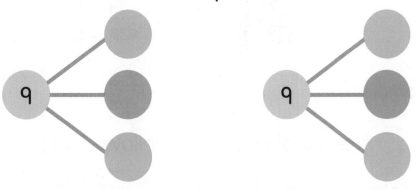

b Find three numbers that make 10.
Think of two more ways to do this.

## Maths Journal

**5** Look at the picture.
Think of two number bonds.

**Example**

[    ] red stool and [    ] yellow stools

make [    ] stools.

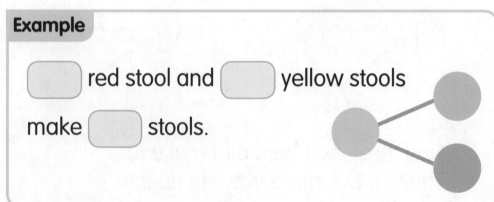

# Put On Your Thinking Caps!

**6** How many beads are hidden?

**a** There are 6 beads altogether under the two cups.

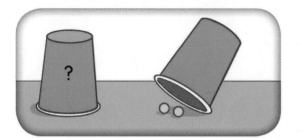 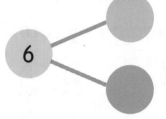

**b** There are 8 beads altogether under the two cups.

 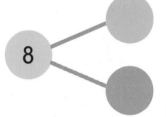

**c** There are 10 beads altogether under the three cups.

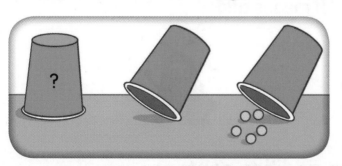 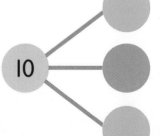

Practice Book IA, p.35 | Practice Book IA, p.36

# 3 Addition within 10

## Let's Learn!

**Ways to add**

### Adding by counting on

   6 + 2 = ?

6

Count on from the greater number.
6, **7**, **8**.

6 + 2 = 8

part  part  whole

+ is called **plus**.
It means **add**.

= means **equals**.

6 + 2 = 8 is an **addition sentence**.
It says **six plus two equals eight**.

**2** Count on from the greater number.

**a**  2 + 5 = ?

5, ⬜ , ⬜

**b**  7 + 3 = ?

7, ⬜ , ⬜ , ⬜

## Activity

**3** Make the number trains below.
Count on from the greater number to find the total
number of 🎲.

**a**  4

5, ⬜ , ⬜ , ⬜ , ⬜

4 + 5 = ⬜

**b**

⬜ , ⬜ , ⬜

⬜ + ⬜ = ⬜

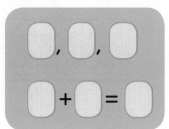

## Activity

**c**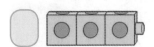

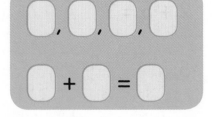

**d**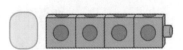

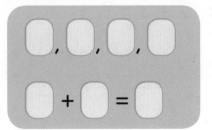

**4** What is 2 more than 7?

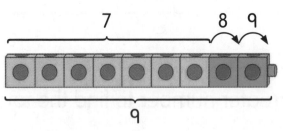

2 added on to 7 is 9.

2 more than 7 is 9.

**5** What is 3 more than 5?

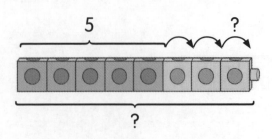

5, [ ], [ ], [ ]

3 more than 5 is [ ].

# Game

**Players:** 3
**You will need:**
• Two sets of number cards

**6** **Card fun!**

How to play:

**1** Make two sets of cards.

Set A

| 1 | 2 | 3 | 0 |

| 1 | 2 | 3 |

Set B

| 1 | 2 | 3 | 4 | 5 |

| 6 | 7 |

**2** Player 1 picks a card from Set A.

**3** Player 2 picks a card from Set B.

**4** Player 3 adds the numbers on the cards.

**5** Players 1 and 2 check the answer.

$5 + 3 = 8$    Correct!

**6** Players get one point for each correct answer. Take turns to pick cards and add the numbers.

Play six rounds. The player with the most points wins.

Practice Book 1A, p.41

## Adding with number bonds

Number bonds can help you add.

How many penguins are there altogether?

3 + 5 = ?

$$3 + 5 = 8$$

How many toys are there altogether?

$$2 + 6 = \boxed{\phantom{00}}$$

**9** How many sheep are there altogether?

part **3**   whole

**7**

part **4**

4 added on to 3 gives 7.

$3 + 4 = 7$

**10** How many bread rolls are there altogether?

**7**

**9**

**2**

☐ added on to ☐ gives ☐.

☐ + ☐ = ☐

Practice Book IA, p.45

33

# Let's Learn!

## Making up addition stories

1

There are 5 ducks in a pond.
4 ducks get into the pond.
There are 9 ducks altogether.

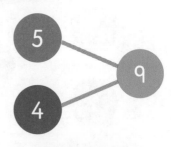

5 + 4 = 9

**2** Look at the pictures.
Make up addition stories.

**a**

2 big teddy bears

5 small teddy bears

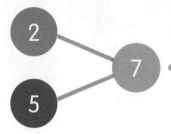

$2 + 5 = 7$

There are ▢ teddy bears altogether.

**b**

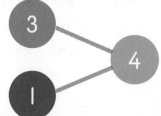

$3 + 1 = 4$

Home Maths

Ask your child to make up addition stories about everyday situations around the home. For example, "There are 2 apples and 5 oranges. There are 7 pieces of fruit altogether."

Practice Book IA, p.51

# Let's Learn!

## Solving word problems

**1**

6 girls are playing football.
3 boys are playing football with them.
How many children are playing football altogether?

> 6 + 3 = 9

9 children are playing football altogether.

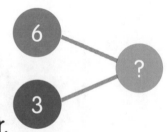

**2** Millie has 3 red flowers.
She has 4 purple flowers.
How many flowers does Millie have altogether?

▢ + ▢ = ▢

Millie has ▢ flowers altogether.

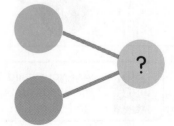

**3** Peter makes 4 cakes.
He makes 5 more cakes.

How many cakes does Peter make altogether?

$4 + 5 = 9$

Peter makes 9 cakes altogether.

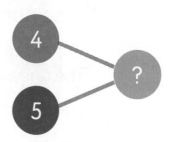

**4**

Ruby has no apples on her plate.
Tai puts 5 apples on Ruby's plate.
How many apples does Ruby have now?

$$\boxed{\phantom{0}} + \boxed{\phantom{0}} = \boxed{\phantom{0}}$$

Ruby has ☐ apples now.

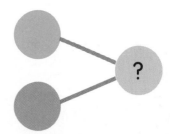

Practice Book IA, p.55

# Put On Your Thinking Caps!

5 Copy the boxes. Fill in the [ ] with 1, 2, 3, 4, 6 or 7. Use each number only once.

Then find the missing number in [ ] , [ ] and [ ] .

These numbers should be 10 or less than 10.

The answer in [ ] should be greater than the answer in [ ] .

The answer in [ ] should be smaller than the answer in [ ] .

[ ] + [ ] = [ ]

[ ] + [ ] = [ ]

[ ] + [ ] = [ ]

There is more than one correct answer.

Practice Book 1A, p.57      Practice Book 1A, p.59

# Subtraction within 10

**Let's Learn!**

## Ways to subtract

### *Subtracting by taking away*

**1** There are 9 spiders. Cross out 6 spiders.

Crossing out 6 spiders means you are taking away 6 spiders.

3 spiders are left.

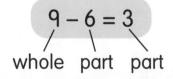

9 – 6 = 3

whole  part  part

– is called **minus**. It means **subtract**.

9 – 6 = 3 is a **subtraction sentence**. It says **nine minus six equals three**.

**2** Look at the pictures.
Find the missing numbers.

**a**

$8 - 3 = \boxed{\phantom{0}}$

**b**

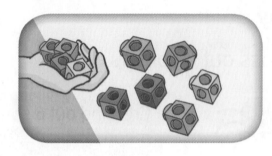

$10 - \boxed{\phantom{0}} = \boxed{\phantom{0}}$

**3** What is 2 less than 6?

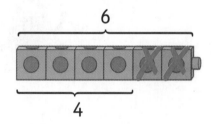

$6 - 2 = 4$

2 less than 6 is 4.

2 taken away from 6 is 4.

**4** What is 5 less than 8?

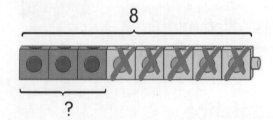

$8 - 5 = \boxed{\phantom{0}}$

5 less than 8 is $\boxed{\phantom{0}}$.

## Subtracting by counting on

**5** There are 9 flies.
6 flies are stuck in a web.
How many flies are still flying?

$9 - 6 = ?$
Count on from the smaller number: 6.
Stop at 9.

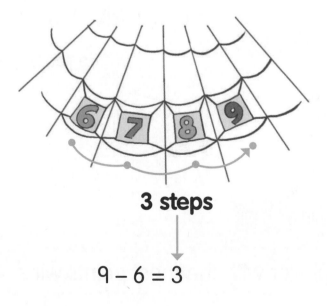

**3 steps**

$9 - 6 = 3$

6, 7, 8, 9

# Game

### 6 What's hidden?

**Players:** 3 to 4
**You will need:**
• 10 cubes

How to play:

**1** Player 1 chooses a number of  and shows them to the other players.

**2** Then player 1 hides some of the .

**3** The other players write the number of  player 1 hid by counting on.

**4** Player 1 checks their answers. Players get one point for each correct answer. Take turns to play.

There were 8. Now there are 5.

5, **6, 7, 8**
You hid 3 !

Correct!

Play four rounds. The player with the most points wins.

**7** Subtract the numbers. Count on from the smaller number.

**a** 8 – 6 = ☐               **b** 6 – 3 = ☐

**c** 10 – 7 = ☐              **d** 9 – 5 = ☐

## *Subtracting by counting back*

**8** 9 – 2 = ?
Start from the greater number, 9.
Count back 2 steps.

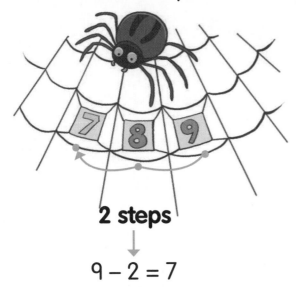

9, 8, 7

**2 steps**
↓
9 – 2 = 7

**9** Subtract the numbers.
Count back from the greater number.

**a** 7 – 2 = ☐               **b** 9 – 3 = ☐

**c** 8 – 3 = ☐               **d** 10 – 3 = ☐

Home Maths — Play Hit 1! The first player begins with 10 and counts back up to 3 steps. The players take turns to count back. The player who says 1 wins.

Practice Book 1A, p.61

## Subtracting with number bonds

Number bonds can help you subtract.

**10** There are 9 bean bags altogether.
How many bean bags does Ruby have on her head?

$9 - 4 = ?$

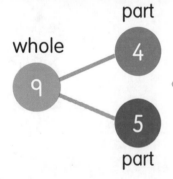

part

whole

$9 - 4 = 5$

part

**11** There are 10 apples altogether.
How many are green?

$10 - 1 = ?$

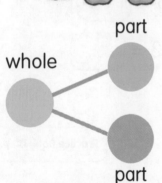

part

whole

$10 - 1 = \boxed{\phantom{0}}$

part

**12** There are 6 sandwiches altogether.
How many are left on the plate?

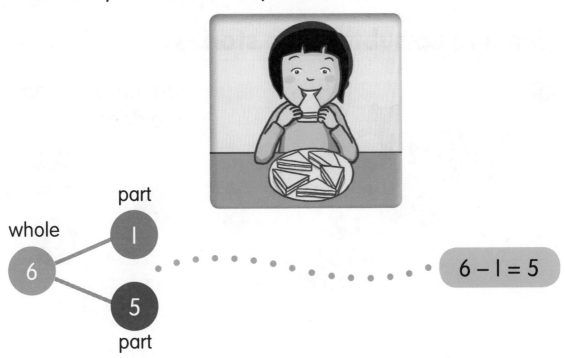

whole

part

6

1

5

part

6 − 1 = 5

**13** There are 10 cats altogether.
How many are not playing?

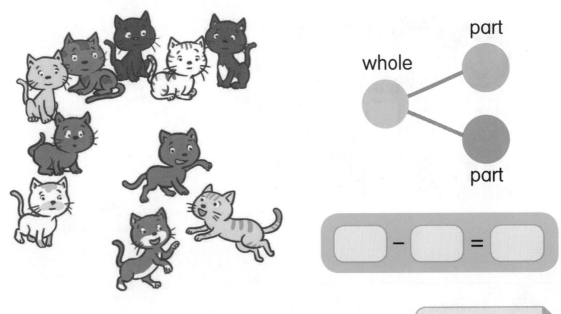

whole

part

part

☐ − ☐ = ☐

Practice Book IA, p.67

# Let's Learn!

## Making up subtraction stories

**1**

There are 7 animals.
4 are dogs.

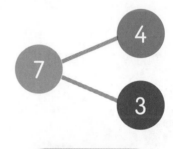

$$7 - 4 = 3$$

3 are cats.

**2** Look at the picture.
Make up a subtraction story.

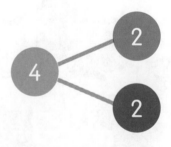

$$4 - 2 = 2$$

**Home Maths**  Encourage your child to make up subtraction
stories about their favourite animals.

Miya has 10 carrot sticks.
She gives Hardeep 2 carrot sticks.

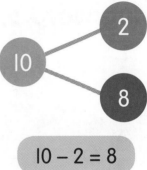

$$10 - 2 = 8$$

Miya has 8 carrot sticks left.

**4** Look at the pictures.
Make up a subtraction story.

8 − ⬜ = ⬜

Practice Book IA, p.73

# Let's Learn!

## Solving word problems

**1**

Jack and Farha have 9 marbles altogether.
Jack has 7 marbles.
How many marbles does Farha have?

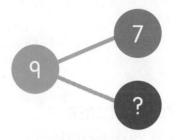

$$9 - 7 = 2$$

Farha has 2 marbles.

**2** There are 10 slices of pizza on a plate.
Ella takes some slices.
There are 6 slices left.
How many slices does Ella take?

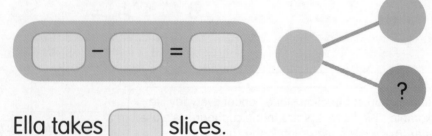

Ella takes ⬚ slices.

There are 7 rabbits.
4 rabbits are playing.
The rest are sleeping.
How many rabbits are sleeping?

$7 - 4 = 3$

3 rabbits are sleeping.

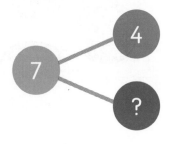

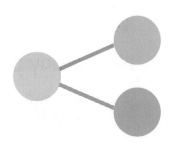

Tai has 9 balloons.
2 balloons pop.
How many balloons are left?

 balloons are left.

Practice Book IA, p.77

# Let's Learn!

## Making a family of number sentences

**1**

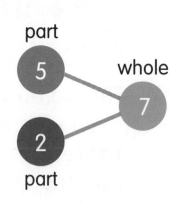

How many balls of string are yellow?

7 − 2 = 5

How many balls of string are blue?

7 − 5 = 2

How many balls of string are there altogether?

2 + 5 = 7   or   5 + 2 = 7

. . . . . . . . . . . . . . . . . . . . . . . . . . . . . . . . . . . . . . . . . . . .

7 − 2 = 5    7 − 5 = 2    2 + 5 = 7    5 + 2 = 7

These make a family of number sentences.

**2** Look at the picture.
Make up a family of number sentences.

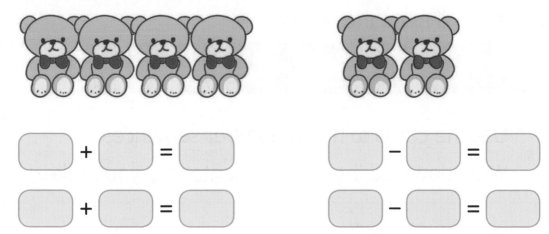

◯ + ◯ = ◯          ◯ − ◯ = ◯

◯ + ◯ = ◯          ◯ − ◯ = ◯

**3** Look at the pictures.
Make up a family of number sentences.

**a**

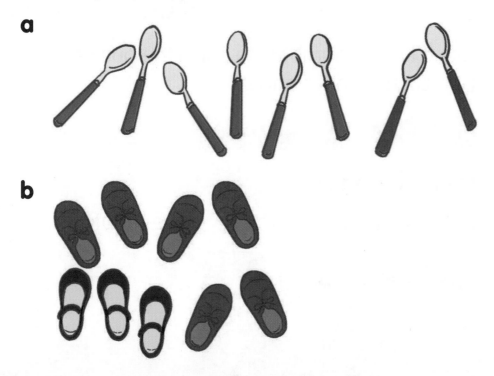

**b**

Home
Maths

Put counters (or coloured pegs, or pieces of coloured paper)
into 2 groups. Each group should have 2 colours and not
more than 10 counters. Ask your child to look at the groups and
make up two families of number sentences. Remember that the
numbers should add up to 10 or less.

Practice Book IA, p.79

## Let's Explore!

**4** You will need these cards.

| 2 | 3 | 6 | 8 | 9 | 10 | + | − | = |

Use the cards to make number sentences.

Write down all the number sentences you make.

## Put On Your Thinking Caps!

**5** **a** Use all these numbers to solve the puzzle.
Use each number once.

1   2   5   6   8   9   10

➜ and ⬇ mean =.

(Hint: The number in the ⬭ is the greatest.)

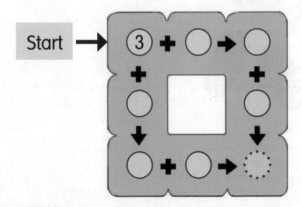

Start ➜ ③ ✚ ◯ ➜ ◯
✚          ✚
◯          ◯
⬇          ⬇
◯ ✚ ◯ ➜ ⬭

# Put On Your Thinking Caps!

**b** Use all these numbers to solve the puzzle.
Use each number once.

2  3  4  5  6  7  8

→ and ↓ mean =.

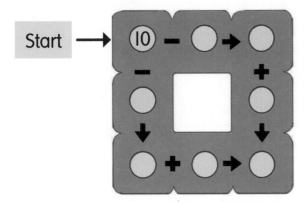

Start

Practice Book IA, p.81     Practice Book IA, p.84

**Let's Learn!**

## Getting to know shapes

**1** Trace these shapes with your finger.
How many sides does each shape have?

circle

triangle

square

rectangle

These are circles.

These are triangles.

These are squares.

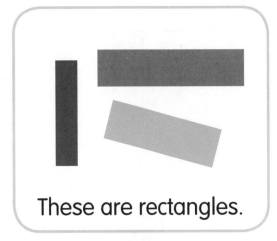
These are rectangles.

How are squares and rectangles different?

③ Which shapes are not squares? How do you know?

## Activity

**4** You will need these shapes.

Group them into types of shape.
Are there other ways to group them?

Practice Book IB, p.5

# Let's Learn!

## Making pictures from shapes

**1** Here are 2 rectangles, 2 triangles and a square.

I made a picture like this.

I made a picture like this.

2 This picture is made up of many shapes.

How many of these shapes can you find?

| Shape | How many? |
|---|---|
| Triangles | |
| Rectangles | |
| Squares | |
| Circles | |

 **Home Maths** Encourage your child to identify shapes around the house or in your area, for example, at the park, at the library, or at the supermarket.

# Activity

**3** Make a picture using paper shapes.

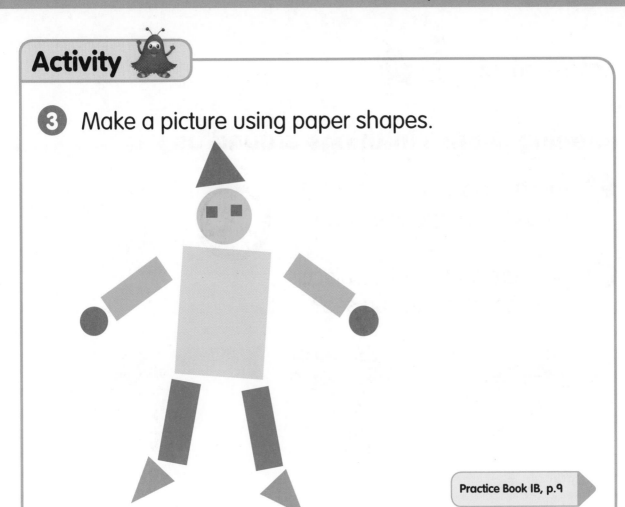

Practice Book 1B, p.9

# Let's Explore!

**4** You will need these shapes.

Make two different pictures using all of these shapes.

 **Home Maths** Ask your child to use shapes to make lots of different pictures. Encourage your child to use a variety of shapes.

59

# Let's Learn!

## Seeing shapes in things around us

**1** This is a clock.
It has the shape of a circle.

**2** Here are some other objects.
What shapes can you see?

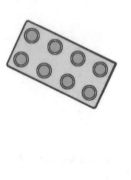
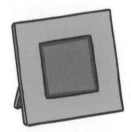

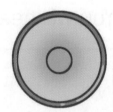

## Activity

**3** Look around your classroom and school.

**a** Name three things that have the shape of a circle.

**b** Name three things that have the shape of a rectangle.

**c** Name three things that have the shape of a triangle.

**d** Name three things that have the shape of a square.

**4** Look at this cereal box.
What shapes can you see?

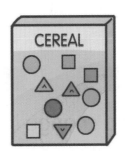

**5** Look at this picture.
What shapes can you see?

**Home Maths** Ask your child to identify shapes in objects around the house. Ask these questions: "What shapes can you see?", "Do you see objects that have more than one shape?", "What are these objects?"

Practice Book 1B, p.15

# Let's Learn!

## Getting to know patterns

**1** These are patterns.

There is a change in shape.

This pattern repeats.

There is a change in size.

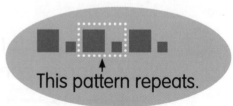
This pattern repeats.

Blue, red, blue, red!

There is a change in colour.

**2** Complete the patterns.

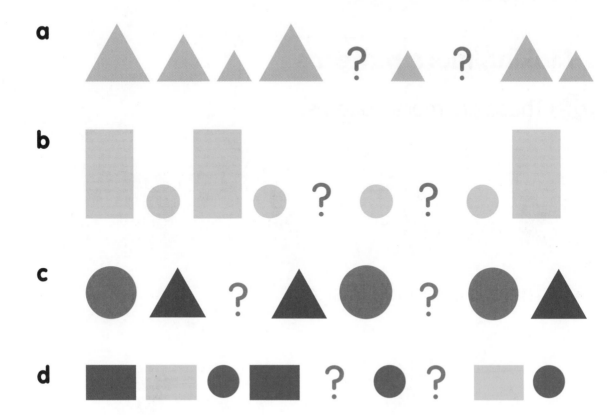

a

b

c

d

**Activity**

**3** Make a pattern using two shapes.
Ask a friend what comes next in the pattern.

Practice Book 1B, p.19

**Home Maths** There are patterns all around us at home, for example on curtains, wrapping paper, clothes and tiles. Ask your child to look around and see how many patterns they can identify.

63

# Let's Learn!

## Making more patterns

**1** These are more patterns.

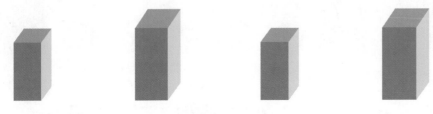

There is a change in size.

There is a change in colour.

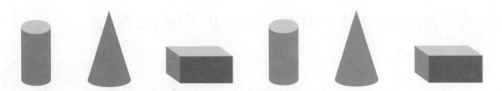

There is a change in object.

**2** What comes next?

**a**

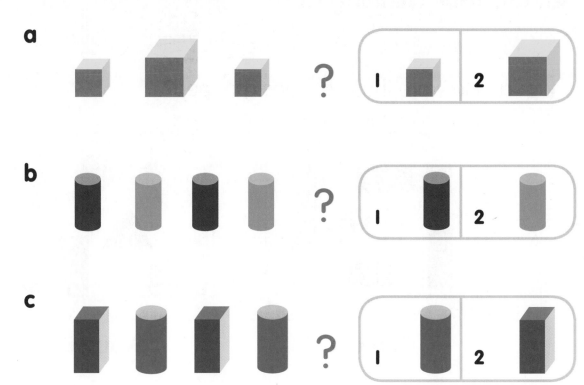

**b**

**c**

**Activity**

**3** You will need these objects.

Make your own patterns.
Ask a friend to show what comes next.

Practice Book IB, p.25

# Put On Your Thinking Caps!

**4**  **a**  How are these shapes grouped?

**Group A**                    **Group B**

**b**  What comes next?

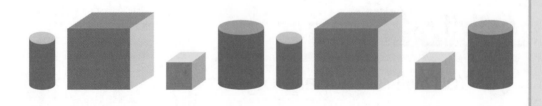

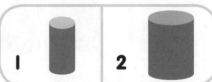

Practice Book IB, p.27        Practice Book IB, p.3I

# Unit 6 Ordinal Numbers

**Let's Learn!**

## Knowing ordinal numbers

**1** There are 5 thirsty children.

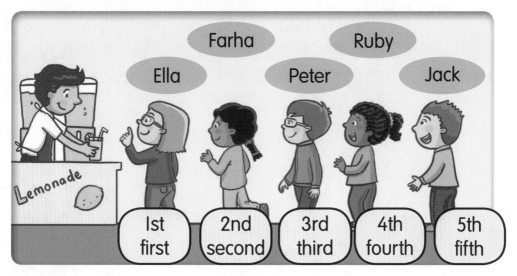

Farha    Ruby

Ella    Peter    Jack

| 1st first | 2nd second | 3rd third | 4th fourth | 5th fifth |

Ella is **before** Farha .

Peter is **after** Farha .

Farha is **between** Ella **and** Peter .

Describe the positions of Ruby and Jack using these words:

before    after

between

**2**

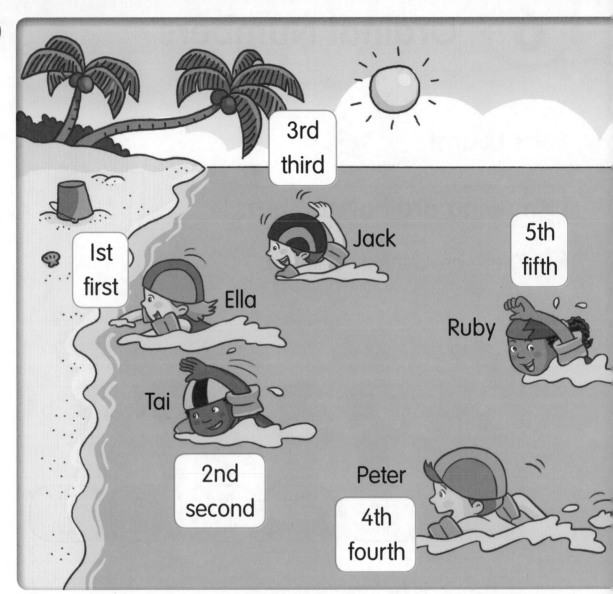

**a** Which children are before Ruby?

**b** Who will be first to the beach?

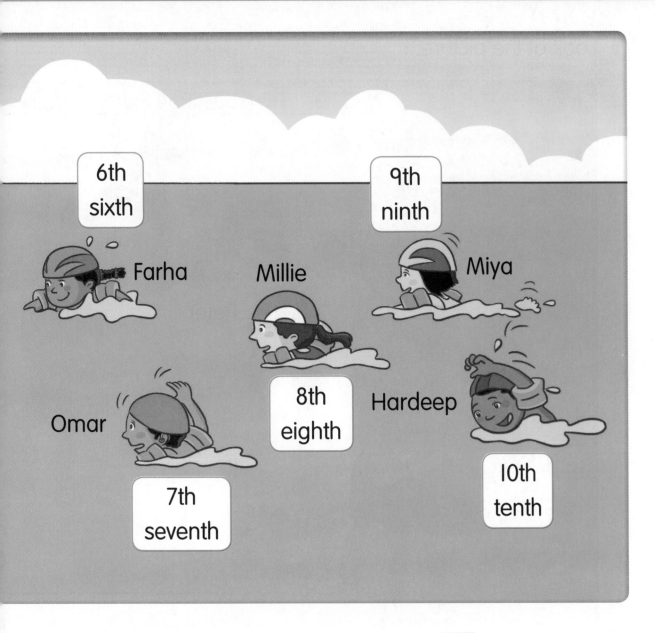

c   Which children are after Millie?

d   Who will be last to the beach?

**3** Look at the picture.

**a**   How many children are climbing the wall?

**b**   Who is Ist?

**c**   Who is last?

**d**   Who is 2nd?

Tai

Millie

Jack

**e** Who is 4th? ⬡

**f** Where is Millie? ⬡

**g** Who is just after Millie? ⬡

**h** Who is just before Ella? ⬡

**4** Look at the picture.

**a** Is anyone at home on the ground floor? ☐

**b** Which floor is the cat on? ☐

**c** Which floor is the man on? ☐

**d** Which floor has the flowers? ☐

**e** Which floor has the bird? ☐

**f** Which floor has the goldfish? ☐

**g** Which animal is on the second floor? ☐

**h** What is the girl on the second floor doing? ☐

**Home Maths** Remind your child that the first floor is the floor above the ground floor.

Practice Book IB, p.33

# Let's Learn!

## Naming left and right positions

The T-shirt is first from the **left**.
The dress is second from the left.

The T-shirt is fifth from the **right**.
It is also last from the right.

The towel is third from the left.
It is also third from the right.

The jeans are between the towel and the skirt.

**2**

Peter    Farha    Ella    Miya    Omar

Left

Peter is **next to** Farha.
Ella is also next to Farha.

Peter is 1st from the left.
He is also 10th or last from the right.

Farha is 2nd from the left.
She is also 9th from the right.

Ruby    Tai    Millie    Hardeep    Jack

Right

**a** Who is last from the left? ☐

**b** Who is 7th from the right? ☐

**c** Who is between Miya and Ruby? ☐

**d** Who is next to Jack? ☐

Practice Book IB, p.39

## Let's Explore!

**3** You will need a set of 9 blue cards and I red card.

**1** Shuffle the cards.
Arrange the cards in a row.

**2** Count and record the following in a chart.
What is the position of the red card from the left?
What is the position of the red card from the right?

| No. | Position of red card from the left | Position of red card from the right | ☐ + ☐ |
|-----|-----|-----|-----|
| I | ☐ | ☐ | ☐ |
| 2 | ☐ | ☐ | ☐ |
| 3 | ☐ | ☐ | ☐ |
| 4 | ☐ | ☐ | ☐ |

**3** Shuffle the cards.
Repeat the activity.
Write your answers in a chart.

The total number of cards is 10.

The answer in the ☐ is always ☐ more than the total number of cards.

# Put On Your Thinking Caps!

**4** Put the people and objects in the correct order.

**a** Ruby, Jack and Miya are in a row.
Ruby is last.
Jack is not 2nd.

| | | |
|---|---|---|
| 1st | | 3rd |

Who is in the middle?
How do you know?

**b** Hardeep plants 4 flowers in a row.
The lily is not 2nd from the left.
The daisy is between the rose and the sunflower.
The sunflower is 1st from the right.

Left                                           Right

Which flower is 3rd from the right?
How do you know?

# Put On Your Thinking Caps!

**5** **a** Omar counts the number of children in his group.
Millie is the 4th child from the right.
She is also the 2nd child from the left.
How many children are there in Omar's group?

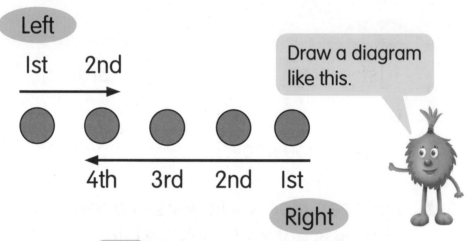

Draw a diagram like this.

There are ☐ children in the group.

**b** Ella arranges 10 beads in a row.
There is only one red bead.
She puts it 6th from the right.
Ella counts from the left.
What position is the red bead in?

Draw a diagram or act this out with your friends.

Practice Book IB, p.43      Practice Book IB, p.44

Let's Learn!

## Counting to 20

### Counting on from 10

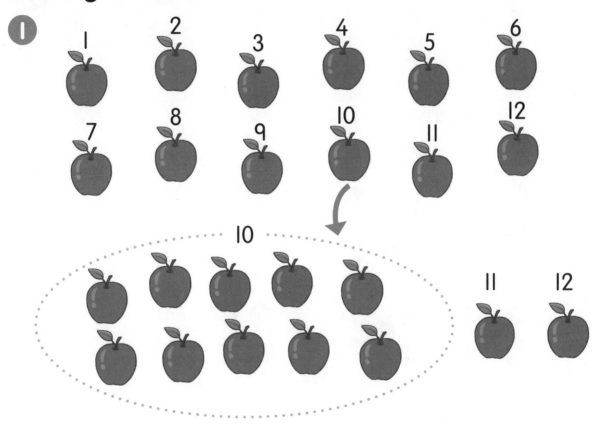

It is easier to count on: 10, **11**, [ ]

**2** Count on from 10.

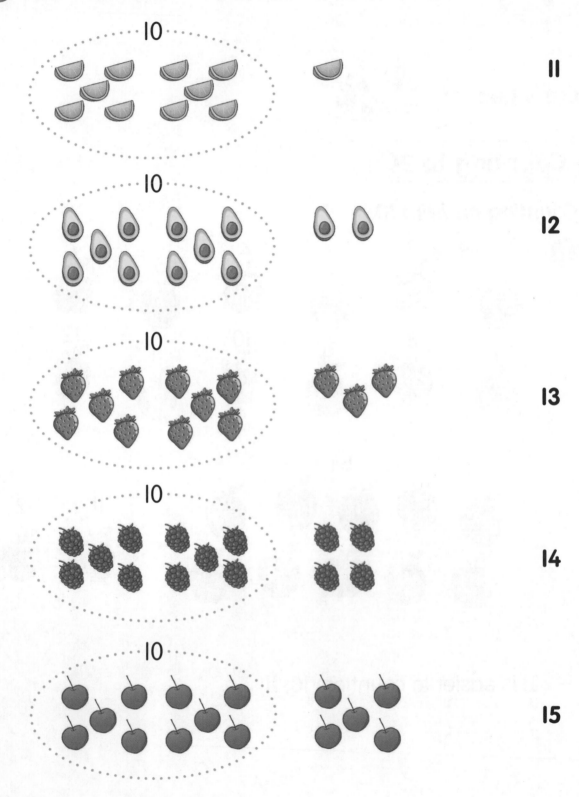

10

11

10

12

10

13

10

14

10

15

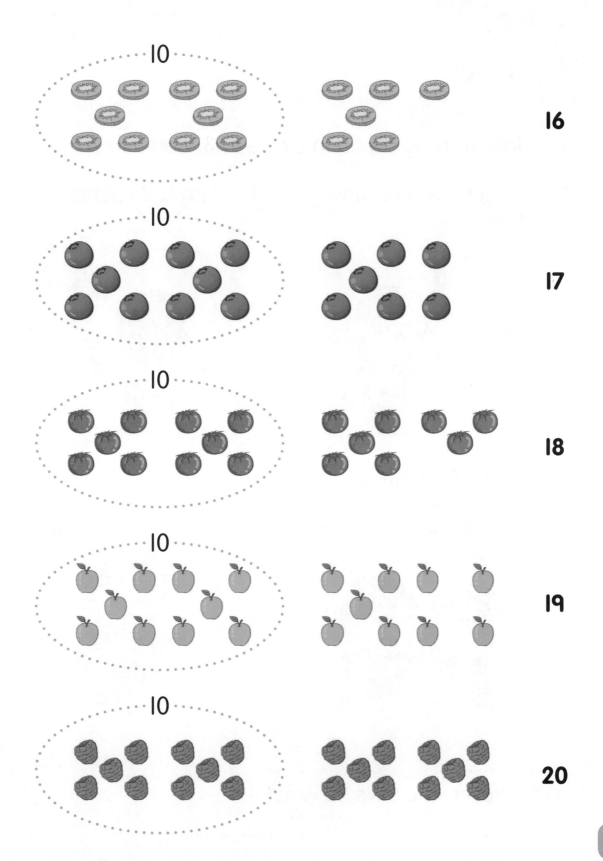

10    16

10    17

10    18

10    19

10    20

## Game

Players: 3

**3** **Hit 20!**

How to play:
Take turns to count on by 1, 2 or 3. Count to 20.

**1** Player 1 starts counting from 1.

**2** Player 2 counts on.

**3** Player 3 counts on.

The player who says 20 wins!

**4** First make ten.
Then count on.

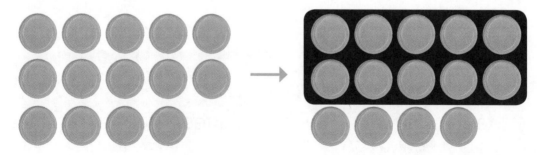

10 and 4 make 14.

$10 + 4 = 14$

**5**

**10** and **1** make **11**.

$10 + 1 = 11$

**10** and **7** make ⬚.

$10 + 7 = $ ⬚

**10** and **10** make ⬚.

$10 + 10 = $ ⬚

## Reading number words 10 to 20

**6** Look at the number.
Read the word.

| 10 | 11 | 12 | 13 | 14 | 15 |
|----|----|----|----|----|----|
| ten | eleven | twelve | thirteen | fourteen | fifteen |

| 16 | 17 | 18 | 19 | 20 |
|----|----|----|----|----|
| sixteen | seventeen | eighteen | nineteen | twenty |

**7** Give the numbers in words.

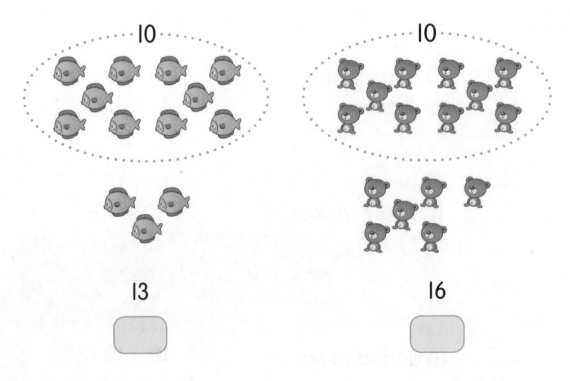

**8** Find the missing numbers.

**a**  1, 2, 3, 4, 5, 6, 7, 8, 9, ☐

**b**  10 and 4 make ☐ .

**c**  10 and 3 make ☐ .

**d**  10 and 6 make ☐ .

**e**  10 and 7 make ☐ .

**f**  10 and 9 make ☐ .

**g**  2 + 10 = ☐

**h**  4 + 10 = ☐

**i**  10 + 3 = ☐

**j**  10 + 8 = ☐

Practice Book 1B, p.51

# Let's Learn!

## Place value

**1**

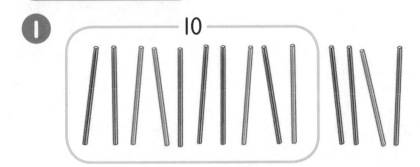

| Tens | Ones |
|------|------|
| 1    | 4    |

14 = 1 ten 4 ones

**2**

| Tens | Ones |
|------|------|
|      |      |

12 = ☐ ten ☐ ones

**3**

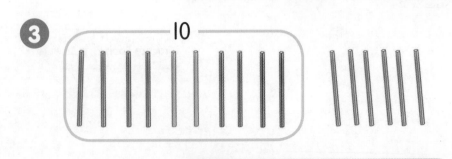

| Tens | Ones |
|------|------|
|      |      |

16 = ☐ ten ☐ ones

**4**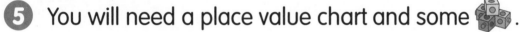

13 = 1 ten 3 ones

| Tens | Ones |
|------|------|
| 1 | 3 |
|  | |

## Activity

**5** You will need a place value chart and some .

Group the to show these numbers.

**a** 18 **b** 20

Draw ☐ for tens and □ for ones.

**Example**

place value chart

|  | Tens | Ones |
|------|------|------|
| 15 | 1 | 5 |
| | ☐ | □ □<br>□ □<br>□ |

Practice Book IB, p.57

# Let's Learn!

**Compare**

**1** Set A

12

Set B

10

Set A has 2 more than Set B.

Set B has 2 fewer than Set A.

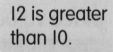
12 is greater than 10.

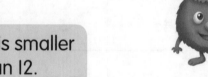
10 is smaller than 12.

**2** Count the number of tennis balls in each set.

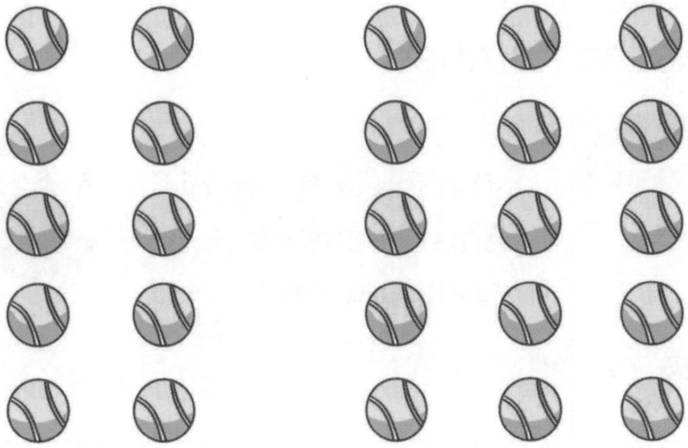

Set A

Set B

Which set has more balls?

How many more?

Which set has fewer balls?

How many fewer?

What is the missing number in each ⬚ ?

⬚ is greater than ⬚ .

⬚ is smaller than ⬚ .

**3** Compare 13 and 15.
Which number is greater?
How much greater is the number?

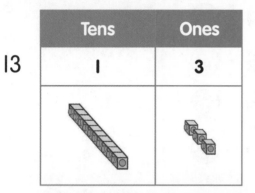

13

| Tens | Ones |
|---|---|
| 1 | 3 |

The tens are equal. This means we compare the ones.

15

| Tens | Ones |
|---|---|
| 1 | 5 |

Compare the ones. 5 is greater than 3.

15 is greater than 13 by 2.

**4** Which number is greater?
How much greater?

**a** 18    15

**b** 19    17

**5** Which number is smaller?
How much smaller?

**a** 16    12

**b** 16    13

**6** Compare 14, 11 and 16.

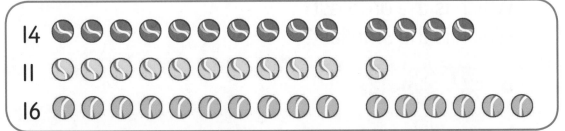

| | Tens | Ones |
|---|---|---|
| 14 | 1 | 4 |

The tens are all equal. This means we compare the ones.

| | Tens | Ones |
|---|---|---|
| 11 | 1 | 1 |

| | Tens | Ones |
|---|---|---|
| 16 | 1 | 6 |

Compare the ones. 6 is greater than 4. 4 is greater than 1.

16 is the **greatest** number.
11 is the **smallest** number.

**7** Compare the numbers.
Which is the greatest?
Which is the smallest?

a (10) (17) (12)

b (19) (14) (11)

c (17) (19) (13)

Practice Book 1B, p.61

**Home Maths** Ask your child to compare the number of items (for example, eggs, apples, yoghurts) in your shopping trolley when you go to the supermarket.

## Let's Explore!

1   Make a number train for the greatest number. Name it Train A.

2   Make a number train for the smallest number. Name it Train B.

3   How many  do you need to take from Train A and give to Train B, so that both trains have the same number of ?

Greatest number = 15

Train A

Smallest number = 11

Train B

Take 2  from Train A. Put them on Train B.

4   Now do the same thing with the following numbers:

a   16   11   19

b   20   12   17

# Let's Learn!

## Order and pattern

**1** Farha uses 🎲 to make a pattern.

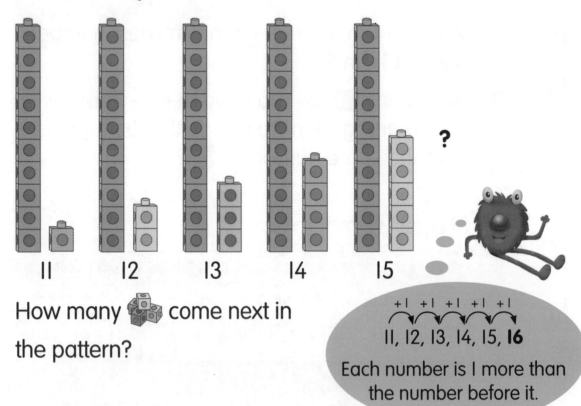

| | | | | |
|---|---|---|---|---|
| 11 | 12 | 13 | 14 | 15 |

How many 🎲 come next in
the pattern?

+1 +1 +1 +1 +1

11, 12, 13, 14, 15, **16**

Each number is 1 more than
the number before it.

**2** Jack uses beads to make a pattern.

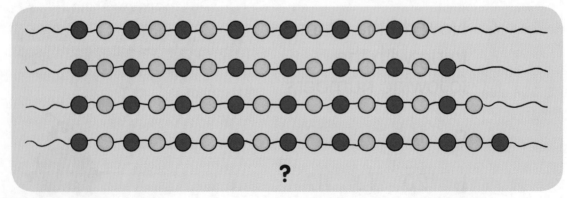

?

How many beads come next in the pattern?

**3** Find the missing numbers.

10, 11, 12, 13, ⬚, ⬚, ⬚

13, **14, 15, 16**!

**4** Find the missing numbers in the number patterns.

**a** 14, 15, 16, 17, ⬚, ⬚, ⬚

**b** 20, 19, 18, ⬚, ⬚, ⬚

**c** 8, 10, 12, ⬚, ⬚, ⬚

**d** 17, 15, 13, ⬚, ⬚, ⬚

**5** What is 1 more than 15?

↓ 1 more

1 more than 15 is 16.

**6** What is 2 more than 17?

↓ 2 more

2 more than 17 is ⬚.

**7** What is 1 less than 16?

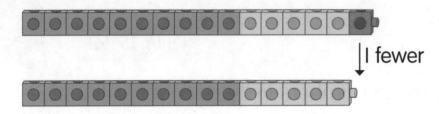

1 less than 16 is 15.

**8** What is 2 less than 20?

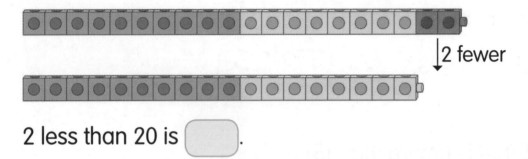

2 less than 20 is ⬚.

**9**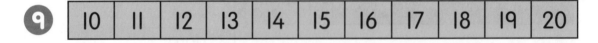

| 10 | 11 | 12 | 13 | 14 | 15 | 16 | 17 | 18 | 19 | 20 |

**a**  2 more than 12 is 14.    **b**  2 more than 18 is ⬚.

**c**  3 more than 10 is ⬚.    **d**  ⬚ is 2 less than 18.

**e**  ⬚ is 2 less than 17.    **f**  ⬚ is 3 less than 20.

**10** Arrange the numbers in order.
Begin with the smallest.

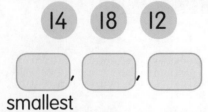

⬚ , ⬚ , ⬚

smallest

Practice Book 1B, p.67

# Put On Your Thinking Caps!

**11** **a** Find the two missing numbers in the pattern.
Put the cards in order.

| 10 | 14 | 16 | 20 |

| ? | ? |

**b** Find the two missing numbers in the pattern.
Put the cards in order.

| 12 | 14 | 15 | 16 |

| ? | ? |

There is more than
one correct answer.

Practice Book IB, p.7I          Practice Book IB, p.73

# Addition and Subtraction within 20

**Let's Learn!**

## Ways to add

### Adding by making 10

**1** Peter has 8 cherries.
Ruby gives him 6 more.

How many cherries does Peter have now?

$8 + 6 = ?$

8 + 6

First make a group of 10 cherries.

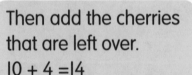

10 4

Then add the cherries that are left over.
$10 + 4 = 14$

Peter has 14 cherries now.

$8 + 6 = 10 + 4$
$= 14$

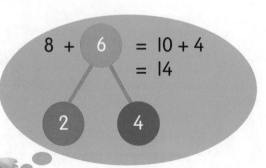

## Activity

**2** Group the straws to make 10.
Then find the answer.

**Example**

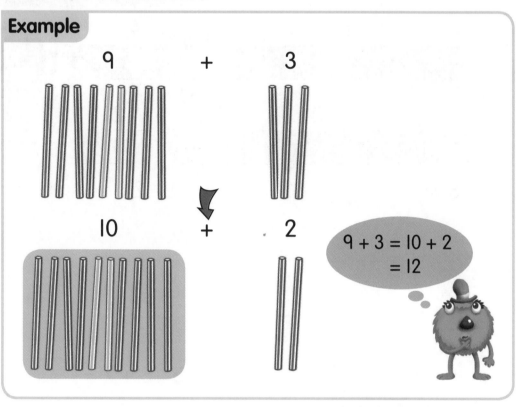

9     +     3

10     +     2

9 + 3 = 10 + 2
    = 12

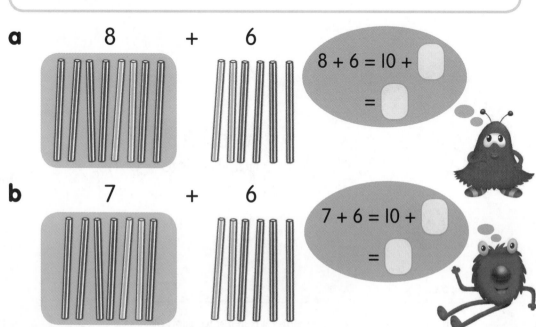

**a**     8     +     6

8 + 6 = 10 + ☐

= ☐

**b**     7     +     6

7 + 6 = 10 + ☐

= ☐

**3** Add by making 10.

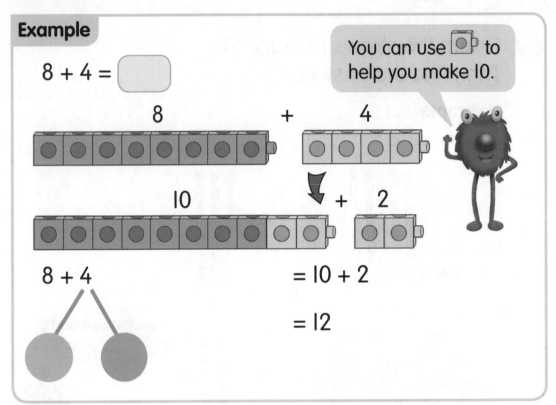

**Example**

$8 + 4 = \boxed{\phantom{00}}$

You can use 🔲 to help you make 10.

8 + 4 = 10 + 2

= 12

**a** $9 + 5 = \boxed{\phantom{00}}$

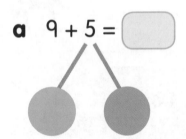

**b** $8 + 7 = \boxed{\phantom{00}}$

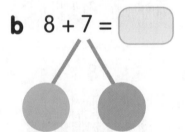

**c** $5 + 7 = \boxed{\phantom{00}}$

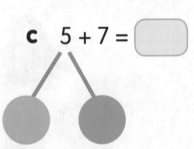

We break the smaller number into 2 parts.

**Home Maths** Help your child to practise adding by making 10 using objects around the house such as beads, buttons or paper clips.

**Practice Book 1B, p.75**

## *Adding by regrouping into tens and ones*

**4** Tai has 16 blue marbles.
His sister gives him 3 yellow marbles.

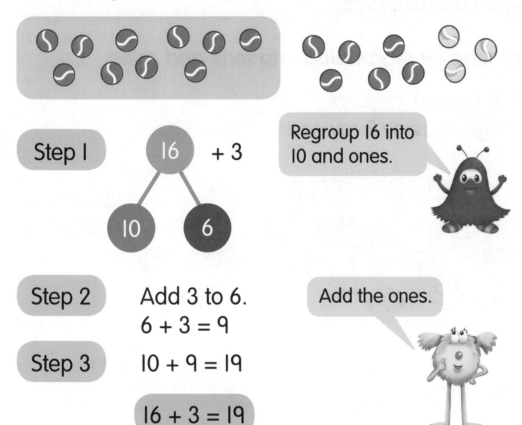

Step 1    16   + 3

Regroup 16 into 10 and ones.

10    6

Step 2    Add 3 to 6.
6 + 3 = 9

Add the ones.

Step 3    10 + 9 = 19

16 + 3 = 19

Tai has 19 marbles altogether.

**5** Regroup the numbers into tens and ones.
Then add the numbers.

**a**   13 + 3 = ☐

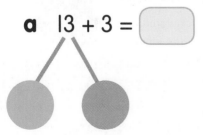

**b**   12 + 7 = ☐

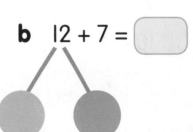

Practice Book 1B, p.79

# Let's Learn!

## Ways to subtract

### Subtracting by regrouping into tens and ones

**1** Peter has 17 toy cars.
He gives away 3 toy cars.

Step 1     17 − 3
           10    7

Regroup 17 into 10 and ones.
17 = 10 + 7

Step 2  Subtract 3 from 7.
        7 − 3 = 4

Subtract the ones.

Step 3  10 + 4 = 14

17 − 3 = 14

Peter has 14 toy cars left.

**2** Regroup the numbers into tens and ones.
Then subtract the numbers.

**a** 17 – 5 = ◻

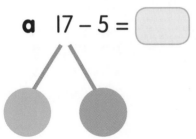

**b** 18 – 3 = ◻

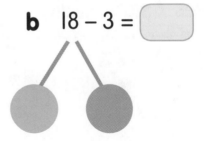

**3** Where is Big Ben?
Subtract to find out.

13 – 3 = ◯ **N**        17 – 6 = ◯ **O**

16 – 2 = ◯ **D**        18 – 5 = ◯ **N**

16 – 1 = ◯ **O**        19 – 3 = ◯ **L**

___ ___ ___ ___ ___ ___
16    11    10    14    15    13

## *More subtraction*

**4** Hardeep makes 12 stars.
He gives 7 stars to Ella.

Step 1    12   − 7
   2    10

Regroup 12 into 10 and ones.
$12 = 10 + 2$

Step 2   $10 − 7 = 3$

We cannot subtract 7 from 2.
We subtract 7 from 10.

Step 3   $2 + 3 = 5$

$12 − 7 = 5$

Hardeep has 5 stars left.

**5** Subtract the numbers.

   **a**   $11 − 3 = \boxed{\phantom{00}}$      **b**   $13 − 6 = \boxed{\phantom{00}}$

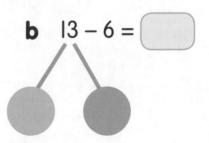

## Game

**6** **Spin and subtract!**

How to play:

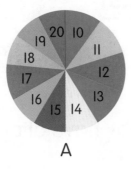

A

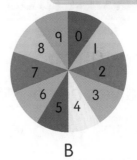

B

**1** Use both spinners to get 2 numbers.

**2** The other 2 players subtract the Spinner B number from the Spinner A number.

**3** The first player with the correct answer wins 1 point. Take turns to spin.

Play six rounds. The player with the most points wins!

Practice Book IB, p.8I

# Let's Learn!

## Solving word problems

**1** Ruby has 9 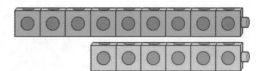.
Farha gives her 6 .
How many does Ruby have altogether?

$$9 + 6 = 15$$

Ruby has 15 altogether.

**2** Omar has 3 counters.
Millie has 14 counters.
How many counters do they
have altogether?

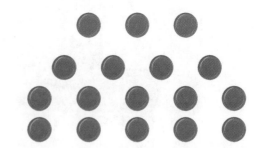

**3** Jack has 16 shells.
He gives Miya 5 shells.
How many shells does Jack
have left?

$$16 - 5 = 11$$

Jack has 11 shells left.

**4** Hardeep has 11 paper clips.
3 of them are blue.
The rest are red.
How many red paper clips are there?

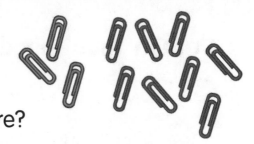

Practice Book 1B, p.89

## Maths Journal

**5** Look at the children around you.

Write an addition story about them.

Write a subtraction story about them.

## Let's Explore!

**6** Make up number sentences using the following numbers. Use addition and subtraction.

You can use each number more than once.

5    6    7    8    9    13    15

How many families of number sentences can you make?

# Put On Your Thinking Caps!

**7** Use all these numbers to solve the puzzle.
Use each number once.

3   4   5   6   7   15

→ and ↓ mean =.

(Hint: The number in the  is the greatest.)

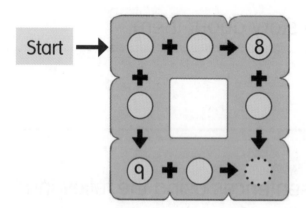

# **Put On Your Thinking Caps!**

8  Use all these numbers to solve the puzzle.
   Use each number once.

   3   4   6   7   8   17

   → and ↓ mean =.

   (Hint: The number in the ⬭ is the greatest.)

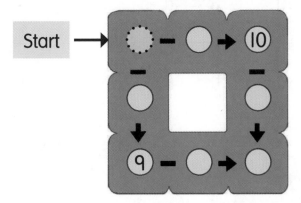

Start →

Practice Book 1B, p.91        Practice Book 1B, p.93

# Length

## Let's Learn!

## Comparing two things

This ladder is tall.

This ladder is taller.

This toy is short.

This toy is shorter.

**2** Stand next to a friend.
Who is taller?
Who is shorter?

**3**

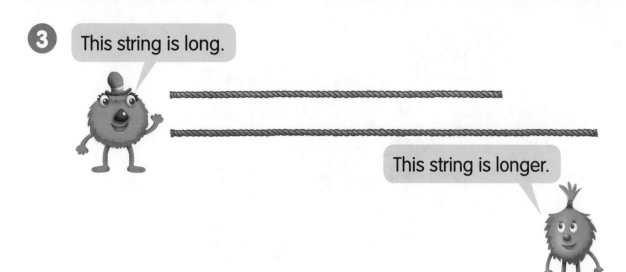

This string is long.

This string is longer.

This string is short.

This string is shorter.

**4** Look at your pencil and your friend's pencil.
Whose pencil is longer?
Whose pencil is shorter?

**5**

**6** Raise your hand.
Now raise it higher.

## Activity

**7** **a** Make a tower with 3 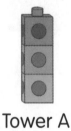.
Name it Tower A.
Make a tower taller than Tower A.
Make a tower shorter than Tower A.

Tower A

**b** Make a number train with 5 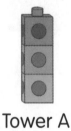.
Name it Train X.
Make a train longer than Train X.
Make a train shorter than Train X.

Train X

**Home Maths** Ask your child to look at things around the house and to compare their heights and lengths. Ask them to say which is taller/longer/shorter/higher. For example, "The stool is shorter than the table." "The tablespoon is longer than the teaspoon."

Practice Book 1B, p.95

# Let's Explore!

 **8**

Ruby and Millie are gardening.
Talk about this picture with a partner.
Use these words.

| | |
|---|---|
| tall | taller |
| long | longer |
| high | higher |
| short | shorter |

# Let's Learn!

## Comparing more things

**1**

Miya      Ethan        Tom

Miya is the **shortest**.

Tom is the **tallest**.

Miya has the **longest** umbrella.

Ethan has the **shortest** umbrella.

The wellington boots are on the **highest** shelf.

**2**

Look at the animals.

Which is the tallest animal?

Which is the shortest animal?

Which animal is longer, the crocodile or the snake?

Which animal is taller than the ostrich?

Which animal is shorter than the zebra?

## Activity

**3** **a** Make four towers.
Place them in order.

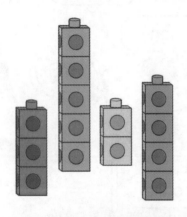

You can start with the tallest or the shortest tower.

Make a tower taller than the tallest tower.

Make a tower shorter than the shortest tower.

**b** Find these in your classroom:

**1** the longest object

**2** the tallest object

**3** the shortest object

**c** Which is the longest word?

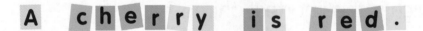

A cherry is red.

Practice Book 1B, p.99

# Let's Learn!

## Using a start line

**1**

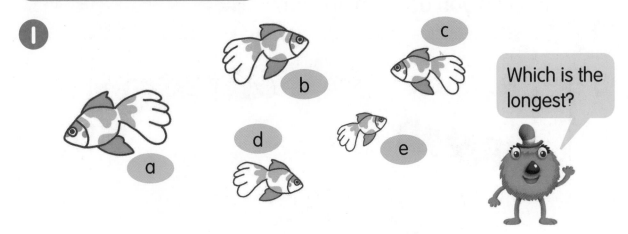

Which is the longest?

Putting objects along a start line helps you to see which is the longest.

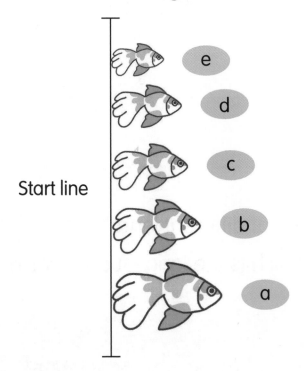

Start line

Which fish is the longest?

2 Look at the strips of paper.
   **a** Which is the longest?

   **b** Which is the shortest?

   What can you use to help you?

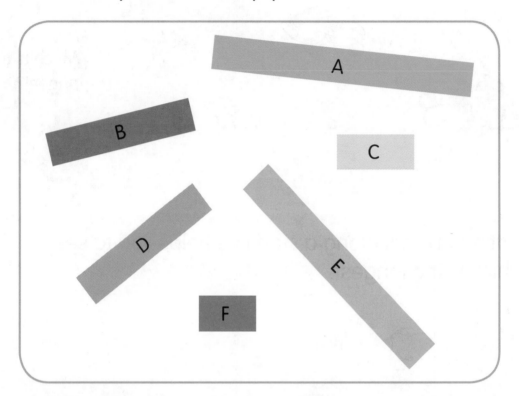

## Activity

3 Cut three strips of paper of different lengths.

   Ask a partner to say which is the longest and which is the shortest.

Practice Book IB, p.103

# Let's Learn!

## Measuring things

**1** Look at the picture.

Make sure all the paper clips are the same length.

The book is **about** 5 paper clips long.
We can also say that its length is about 5 paper clips.

## Activity

**2** Use drinking straws to measure the following:

**a** the teacher's table
**b** your table
**c** your book

Which is the longest?
Which is the shortest?
Is your table longer than the teacher's table?

---

Home
Maths    Explain to your child that we say 'about' when a measurement is not exact.

119

**3** Look at the pictures.

pencil

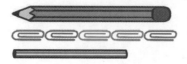

pencil case

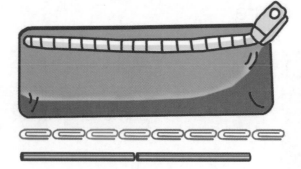

water bottle

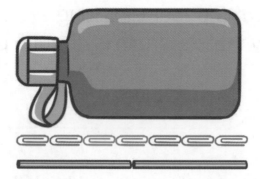

**a** How long is the pencil?

**b** How long is the pencil case?

**c** How long is the water bottle?

**d** Which is the longest?

**e** Is the pencil longer than the pencil case?

## Activity

**4** Work with a partner.

**1** Cut a strip of paper like the one below.

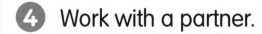

**2** Make 4 more strips of the same length.

**3** Ask your partner to use these strips to measure the length of your arm.

**4** Trace round your foot on a piece of paper.

**5** Use the strips of paper to measure the length of your foot.

My arm is about ⬚ strips of paper long.

My foot is about ⬚ strips of paper long.

## Activity

**5** You will need some strips of paper and paper clips.
Guess how many paper clips long each strip is.
Check by placing paper clips along the strips.
How many of your guesses are correct?

Which strips have the same length?
Which is the longest strip?
Which is the shortest strip?

Put the strips in order from the longest to
the shortest.

Practice Book IB, p.I05

# Let's Learn!

## Finding length in units

**1**  stands for I unit.

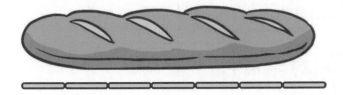

The loaf of bread is about 7 units long.

**2** ⊂⊃ stands for I unit.

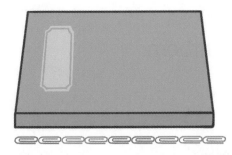

How many units long is this book?

**3** It's bedtime for Jack.

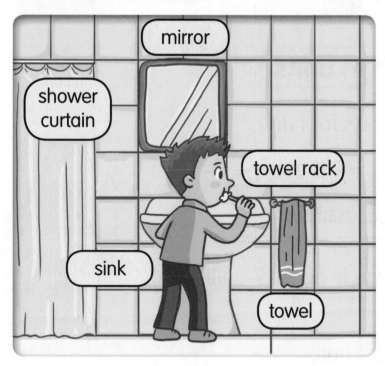

Look at the things in the bathroom.

Each ☐ stands for I unit.

**a** How long is the towel rack?

**b** How tall is the shower curtain?

**c** Is the towel rack longer than the mirror?

**d** Which is shorter, the towel or the towel rack?

## Activity

4 Use 🖉 to measure the objects shown.

Then use / to measure.

Copy the chart. Fill in your answers.

| | Number of 🖉 | Number of / |
|---|---|---|
| Table | | |
| Book | | |
| Pencil | | |

Practice Book 1B, p.109

Explain to your child that using different objects to stand for 1 unit gives different measurements. Remind your child that we use the same object to compare the lengths of 2 different items.

# Put On Your Thinking Caps!

**5** **a** Look at the loaf of bread and the book.

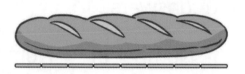

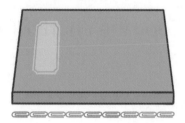

Is the book longer than the loaf of bread? Why?

**b**

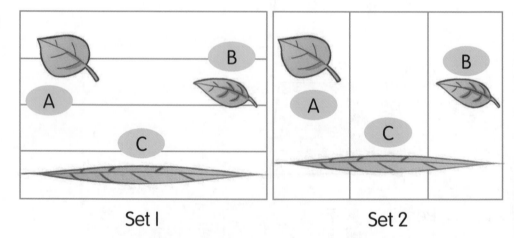

Set 1                                   Set 2

Can you find out how long these leaves are?
Which set of lines should you use? Why?

Practice Book IB, p.II3        Practice Book IB, p.II6

**Published by Marshall Cavendish Education**
Times Centre, 1 New Industrial Road, Singapore 536196
Customer Service Hotline: (65) 6213 9444
Email: tmesales@mceducation.com
Website: www.mceducation.com

Distributed by
**Oxford University Press**
Great Clarendon Street, Oxford,
OX2 6DP, United Kingdom
www.oxfordprimary.co.uk
www.oxfordowl.co.uk

First published 2015
Reprinted 2015, 2016, 2017

ISBN 978-981-01-8860-3

Printed in China

Acknowledgements
Written by Dr Fong Ho Kheong, Chelvi Ramakrishnan and Bernice Lau Pui Wah

UK consultants: Carole Skinner, Simon d'Angelo and Elizabeth Gibbs

Cover artwork by Daron Parton

The authors and publisher would like to thank all schools and individuals who
helped to trial and review Inspire Maths resources.